Contents

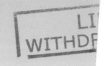

Some words are shown in bold, **like this.** You can find out what they mean by looking in the glossary.

Cargo jets

These planes don't carry passengers. Their large rear doors open to easily load **cargo**.

Even full-size vehicles fit on these large jets.

Hot air balloons

Hot air balloons use air to fly. A flame heats up the air that **expands** the balloon. Riders stand in a basket called a **gondola**.

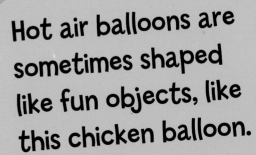

gondola →

Hot air balloons are sometimes shaped like fun objects, like this chicken balloon.

The first hot air balloon
was flown in 1783.

Airships

A gas called **helium** is blown into an airship to make it fly. It's just like blowing up a balloon!

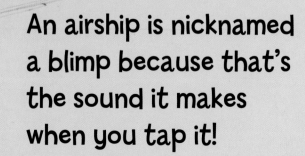

An airship is nicknamed a blimp because that's the sound it makes when you tap it!

Drivers and passengers sit in a
cabin underneath the airship.

Chinooks

The Chinook is a large helicopter. It carries **troops** and supplies to battlefields.

The Chinook has two sets of spinning **rotor blades**. Most helicopters only have one.

Chinooks have two engines.
If one engine stops working,
the helicopter can still fly
with just the other one.

Super jumbo

This **double-decker** is the largest passenger plane in the world. More than 800 people fit on its two floors.

You can find beds and a staircase on board!

Super
Big
Mighty
Size

13

Space station

Astronauts live and work at the *International Space Station.*

Super
Big Mighty
Size

The space station is moving around Earth all the time. It circles Earth once every 90 minutes!

Rockets

Rockets helped to **propel** space shuttles into space.

The Saturn V rocket weighed as much as 400 elephants.

Super

Big

Mighty

Size

The Saturn V rocket helped transport the first astronauts on the Moon.

Space shuttle

A space shuttle carried astronauts into space and back again.

Two huge rockets blasted the shuttle into space.

Space shuttles didn't use engine power to return to Earth. They **glided** back down.

19

Sizing things up

Super Jumbo

Four engines
Two levels
Holds 853 passengers
Wingspan............. 80 metres (262 feet)
Speed................ up to 901 kilometres
(560 miles) per hour

ROYAL AUSTRALIAN AIR FORCE

AIRBUS

Boeing 737

Two engines
One level
Holds 215 passengers
Wingspan . . . . 34 metres (113 feet)
Speed . . . . up to 938 kilometres
(583 miles) per hour

Quiz

How much of a Machine Mega-Brain are you?
Can you match each machine name to its correct photo?

**space station • airship
Chinook • cargo jet**

1

2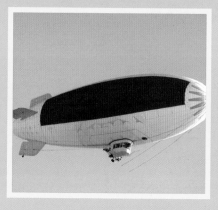

3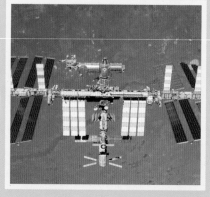

4

Check the answers on the opposite page
to see if you got all four correct.

Glossary

astronaut a crew member of a spacecraft

cargo objects carried by a ship, aircraft, or other vehicle

double-decker a vehicle with two floors

expand to grow larger

glide to move without any effort

gondola the part of an airship in which the crew travels

helium a lightweight, colourless gas that does not burn

propel to move forward

rotor blade a part of a machine with a sharp edge that spins

troop a group of soilders

Find out more

Books

Aircraft (How it Works), Steve Parker (Miles Kelly Publishing Ltd, 2009)

Planes, Rockets and other Flying Machines (Time Shift), Ian Graham (Book House, 2009)

Websites

www.rafmuseum.org.uk/
www.spacecentre.co.uk/

Index